Sad Face

by
Deborah Simmons

FOREWARD

Every now and then, God equips a soldier in the army of the Lord to touch, hold, and heal the hurting hearts of others — even when their pain is foreign to the person healing the pain. Such is the case when Deborah Hughes-Simmons capture and illustrate the very soul of children whose past is tainted with incestuous sexual abuse. Never have I witnessed such empathy, compassion and love as what is seen in the book " Sad Face."

I am convinced that God actually anointed Deborah Hughes-Simmons to write this book so that many quiet, damaged, exploited, hurting children could grasp the courage that it takes to speak up and out about their abuse. It is heart wrenching and breath taking. Most of all, coupled with the wonderful illustrations created by Jeremy Spears, it offers hope, deliverance and true salvation to children that have been hurt, that are still hurting, and even those that on "tomorrow' will be hurting!

It is my prayer that school districts will reach for this book to help the hopeless, and that churches near and abroad will recognize this book as a "must read" for all children, leaders, students, ministers, and teachers.

Having experienced the traumatic episode of sexual abuse, I wept as I read it and grieved for the many years that I could have been helped and healed, had someone taken the time to minister as Deborah Hughes-Simmons did with " Sad Face".

-Dr. Wanda A. Turner
Author, Motivational Speaker

PREFACE

Before the age of 18, one in every four girls and one in every six boys will experience sexual abuse. Their peers, older siblings, relatives or friends will have violated them. It is destroying their spirit and soul.

I am finding out that so many of our adolescent girls and young women carry secrets. Sometimes we may sense the pain, but we don't know what to do or say to help them.

It is time for us to educate ourselves, so that we will be able to stop the abuse.

ACKNOWLEDGEMENTS

Special thanks to Gwen Shorter, Adrienne Hammonds, and Lamont Blackshire for editing and administrative support. I also thank my mother, Dr. Inell Hughes, for being there for me whenever needed.

I dedicate this book to my daughter, Brittney, who was my inspiration for writing it.

I thank my husband, Bishop Esley Simmons, for all his love and support. I love you!

Dr. Deborah Simmons

Hey little girl with the sad, sad eyes,
why do you always look like you're ready to cry?

You don't like to play with the other little girls.
You don't play with dolls; you don't like pretty curls?

What happened to make you so sad?
You always look like you're very, very mad.

Is there some dark secret?
Are you afraid to say?

Did somebody touch you in the wrong way?

Is it about the pain and what happened to you?
Listen little girl, your body belongs to you.

Talk to somebody, you are not alone.
There is somebody you can call on the phone.

Dial 9-1-1 and help will come.

They told you it was a secret, and said you'd better not tell.
It made you not feel very well.

They said you were bad for what you had done.
Then they said, "Don't tell anyone."

You are hurting inside and don't know what to do.
You don't understand what happened to you.

It was a secret, but now you can tell.
You can talk to someone who can help make you well!

Your voice is so soft and you talk so low.
It won't hide your secret, you must know.

You feel so ashamed, but it is not your fault.
Don't be afraid, open your mouth and talk.

Next time they ask you, "What happened today"?

Open your mouth and boldly say:
"I need some help. I've been touched in the wrong way"!

It may have been a brother, uncle, or friend.
You can still tell so your heart can mend.

You can find a number or someone who makes you feel safe.
Stand up little girl and take your place.

You are important and special too.
And we are concerned about what happens to you.

They said you were pretty and you could be rich.
But it only made you feel pretty sick.

Now it is time to take your place.
Heal from the pain; put a smile on your face.

About the Author

He who findeth a wife findeth a good thing . . . Proverbs 18:22

Dr. Deborah C. Simmons was born on August 25, 1953 in Los Angeles, California to the union of Pastor and Mrs. Lester D. Hughes. Deborah is the middle girl of eight children.

Deborah met and married Esley B. Simmons on April 12, 1972. Together they have reared and raised four sons and one daughter. Although excelling at the role of loving wife and mother, Deborah decided to continue to pursue her education. She has an Associate of Science in Math, is a Certified Medical Assistant and has a Juris Doctorate in Law.

One of Deborah's favorite pastimes is writing. She is an accomplished author and has several "soon to be released" children's books.

Debbie, as she is so affectionately called by her husband, is also an ordained Minister of the Gospel. She lives by the Word of God, and carries herself as an example of a "True Lady" and "Woman of God".

ACCOMPLISHMENTS:

California Certified Medical Assistant
Associate Science Degree in Math
Doctorate in Christian Education
Juris Doctorate in Law
Co-Pastor/Founder, South Sacramento Christian Center
Published Author: "Five Days from the Diary of a Demon"

Made in the USA
Monee, IL
04 April 2023

30705675R10017